TWO MANNERS OF LIFE

TITUS CHU

Two Manners of Life
by Titus Chu

First Edition, 1.0: February 2014
PDF & Print on Demand

© 2014 by Titus Chu
ISBN: 978-1-932020-38-0

Distributed by
The Church in Cleveland Literature Service
3150 Warren Road
Cleveland, Ohio 44111

Available for purchase online.
Printed by CreateSpace,
an Amazon.com company.

Download the PDF version of this book at
www.MinistryMessages.org

Please send correspondence by email to
TheEditors@MinistryMessages.org

Published by
Good Land Publishers
Ann Arbor, Michigan

Unless otherwise noted,
Scripture quotations are from the
New American Standard Bible®,
© 1960, 1995
by The Lockman Foundation.

Contents

1

The Origin of the Two Manners of Life

Only Two Choices

The Bible shows us from the very beginning that we can choose from only two possible manners of life. These are portrayed by two trees in the Garden of Eden and then by two lines of descendants from Adam and Eve. In the midst of the Garden of Eden there were two trees: the tree of life and the tree of the knowledge of good and evil (Gen. 2:9). Adam and Eve fell by partaking of the second tree, the tree of knowledge. After they fell, Eve gave birth to two sons, Cain and Abel. These two sons and those who came after them portray two different manners of life corresponding to the two trees: the line of life and the line of knowledge. The principle is the same. The two trees and the two lines represent two distinct manners of life.

We may think that there are many different ways we can live on this earth. For example, we can become doctors, nurses, engineers, plumbers, teachers, or any number of things. We may think we have many options, but in the sight of God we can only belong to one of two lines. We are in the line of life or in the line of the knowledge of good and evil. We can choose from only these two possible manners of life.

Cain—Obeying God's Command

Cain became a tiller of the ground (Gen. 4:2). This was probably because he learned something from his father. Adam likely explained to his sons that after he and Eve fell by eating of the tree of knowledge, God said to them, "Cursed is the ground because of you; in toil you will eat of it all the days of your life....By the sweat of your face you will eat bread" (3:17, 19). Originally, the Garden of Eden was a pleasant and fruitful place, providing everything they needed. But after the fall, the entire earth changed. The ground brought forth thorns and thistles (v. 18). God told Adam that he must now labor on the land to survive. Man could only eat by the toil of his labor and the sweat of his face. Adam must have explained this to his two sons, and this is why Cain became a tiller of the ground. God said to toil on the ground, and Cain was obedient to God's commandment.

Abel—Living according to a Vision

Although Cain was a tiller of the ground according to God's command, he did not have a vision from God. Cain's thought was, "God told us to toil on the ground and eat by the sweat of our brow. Therefore, I must become a farmer."

But Cain's brother Abel was different. Abel saw something higher. Adam probably also told his sons about how, after the fall, he and Eve had clothed themselves with fig leaves. But this did not satisfy God, and they hid from Him. It was not until God slaughtered some animals and made the skin into clothes for them that they were no longer afraid (Gen. 3:7, 21). This became a vision to Abel. He realized that the salvation God had provided man required the death of animals for covering. This caused Abel to become a shepherd. "Abel was a keeper of flocks, but Cain was a tiller of the ground" (4:2). Abel lived according to a vision from God of His salvation.

Command versus Vision

These two lines represent two different manners of life. The line of Cain began with God's command. This line began with the thought, "God said to do it, so I must do it." This is the line of knowledge, which is also the line of religion. However, the line of Abel began with a vision: "I have seen something according to God's desire, and I must live according to this vision." This is the line of life. We must realize that doing what God says is not nearly as high as understanding God's heart. Cain's farming was according to God's command, but Abel's shepherding was according to a vision of God's salvation. As we follow the Lord, we must choose between these two lines.

The Offerings of Cain and Abel

Eventually, Cain and Abel each offered something to God. Their two manners of life resulted in two different offerings. Cain offered something from his farming, "the fruit of the ground," and Abel offered something from his shepherding, "the firstlings of his flock" (Gen. 4:3–4). However, God had no regard for Cain's offering. He only had regard for Abel's offering (vv. 4–5). If Cain had repented, there would have been no further problem. God's enjoyment of Abel's offering was a deep suffering to Cain.

Why didn't God appreciate Cain's offering, and why did God enjoy Abel's offering? We could argue with God, "You were the one who told Adam to farm the land. Cain only did what his father told him to do, but You didn't even have regard for his offering. You only loved Abel's offering. Isn't this unfair?" However, since man fell, no one can come to God except through the way of salvation He has provided. Abel's offering was according to the vision of God's salvation. That is why God had regard for his offering.

When the Lord Jesus came, John the Baptist saw Him and said, "Behold, the Lamb of God who takes away the sin of the world!" (John 1:29). Christ as the Lamb of God was typified by the firstling of the flock that Abel offered. Abel's offering implies that he realized he could only come to God according to God's way of salvation. Abel's offering was according to a vision.

However, God had no regard for Cain's offering because Cain was merely acting according to an objective knowledge of God's commandment. Cain's offering was in the sphere of religion. He offered something to God out of his own work without taking God's salvation. Therefore, his offering did not give him access to God.

The line of Cain is the line of tree of the knowledge of good and evil. Since God had told Adam to labor on the earth for food, Cain became a farmer. This was logical. But when he offered something from the fruit of the ground, God rejected his offering. Abel, however, was not concerned so much for his food. At that time, people didn't even eat meat, so Abel's shepherding had nothing to do with his food supply (Gen. 1:29; 9:3). Nor is there any record that he farmed for food. Probably Abel's only food came from his brother's farming. Abel knew that he must be covered with skins to see God, so he became a shepherd. God regarded Abel's offering and was very satisfied. Both of these sons of Adam did their best to please God by offering something to Him. However, Cain's offering was according to his religious logic, while Abel's offering was according to a vision. These two offerings produced very different results. God rejected one and was pleased with the other.

The Murder of Abel

After God rejected his offering, Cain was so angry and jealous that he slew his own brother (Gen. 4:8). Abel was murdered possibly in the very field where Cain had worked so hard to obey God's commandment. Abel was the first martyr in the Bible and in the whole human race. He was martyred because he saw a vision and lived according to it. He knew that God had told Adam to work on the land and toil with sweat for something to eat. But instead of working on the land for food, Abel became a shepherd and offered the first-lings of his flock to God. This shows that Abel lived according to a high vision of God's salvation. His living was acceptable to God. Abel was then martyred by Cain, the one who lived according to God's commandment.

After the murder, God asked Cain, "Where is Abel your brother?" Cain answered with the famous line, "Am I my brother's keeper?" (v. 9). God responded, "What have you done? The voice of your brother's blood is crying to Me from the ground" (v. 10). God then strengthened the curse on the ground and told Cain that he would be a "vagrant and a wan-derer on the earth" (vv. 11–12). Cain was afraid and said, "Whoever finds me will kill me" (v. 14). God put a mark on Cain for his protection so that no one would kill him. Then Cain went out from God's presence (vv. 15–16).

Seth—The Continuation of Abel

After Abel was murdered and Cain went away, Adam and Eve had another son. "Adam had relations with his wife again; and she gave birth to a son, and named him Seth, for, she said, 'God has appointed me another offspring in place of Abel, for Cain killed him'" (Gen. 4:25). After Cain slew Abel, God appointed another in his place. The death of Abel was necessary for the appointment of Seth. Abel and Seth should be seen as two halves of one person. The first half of this per-son was Abel, who was martyred by Cain. The second half of this person was Seth, who was appointed to carry out God's purpose. Seth represents Abel's continuation. Even though

Abel was dead, Abel's line—the line of life—was continued by Seth and his descendants. From this point on, the Bible records two genealogies representing the two manners of life: the line of Cain and the line of Seth.

Manifested versus Hidden

Even today, there are two manners of life. The first came from Cain. He and his descendants, who raised livestock, produced music, and forged bronze and iron (Gen. 4:20–22), are the basis of all human culture. Raising livestock is related to making a living, producing music is related to entertainment, and forging bronze and iron is related to self-defense. Everything of human culture belongs to one of these three categories. The manner of life represented by Cain permeates all human civilization.

There is a crucial difference between these two manners of life: the first line, the line of Cain, is manifested, while the second line, the line of Abel and Seth, is hidden. Making a living, entertainment, and self-defense are all manifested, but the line of Abel and Seth is hidden. This hidden line is a line of vision.

Living according to Vision

We need to pray, "Lord, I want to be in the line of Abel and Seth and live according to vision." Do we really see the difference between living according to our natural understanding of what pleases God and living according to a vision? For instance, the Bible says that we should love the Lord with all our heart, all our soul, all our mind, and all our strength (Mark 12:30). This is a commandment. Yet our interpretation of this commandment may be very peculiar. We may think, "This means that I need to attend all the church meetings."

This is very good, but it is not enough because such a thought is from Cain's line. We may do things which are appropriate according to God's commandment, yet we may not satisfy God Himself. God is only satisfied when our living is according to the revelation of Jesus Christ.

Our life must be based on vision. Those who do not live according to vision cannot please God in full. When we do things according to our religious logic or culture we are living in the line of the tree of knowledge. But when we do things according to vision, we are living in the proper line, the line of the tree of life. Whatever comes from the line of the tree of knowledge, God will reject; whatever comes from the line of the tree of life, God will accept. There is no third line or middle ground. We should realize that the line of Cain is not limited to things that are evil and corrupt. Cain slew Abel because God was not pleased with Cain's offering. Cain did not begin with murder in his heart. He began by doing exactly what God told him to do, but not according to vision. This is a sober matter. We must be different from Cain. Our desire before the Lord must be to live in the line of life according to the revelation of Jesus Christ.

2

Cain and Abel— Acquisition and Vanity

The Struggle between the Two Lines of Mankind

God portrayed two manners of life when He placed the tree of life and the tree of the knowledge of good and evil in the Garden of Eden. Some people think the second tree is only a tree of evil. Actually, this tree is a tree of knowledge, which includes both good and evil. It is a tree of logic telling us what is good and what is evil. Life is one line, and knowledge or logic is another line.

There are only these two trees or lines for us to live by. We either live according to life or we live according to our understanding of what is good and what is evil. Whenever we do not live in the line of life, our living is automatically decided by our logic. Everyone in the line of knowledge lives according to some form of logic. Our logic may come from our culture, from the teachings of our parents, or even from the Bible itself. When we live according to what is good and what is evil, we are living by our logic. This is different from living according to the line of life.

When Adam fell, all of mankind was brought to the line of the knowledge of good and evil (Rom. 5:18–19). But out of Adam's descendants, the Lord desired to regain what He had lost by bringing man to the line of life. Adam's first two descendants became two lines: the line of Cain and the line of Abel. Cain was on the line of knowledge, and Abel was on the line of life. After Cain killed Abel, Adam had another son named Seth who became the continuation of Abel's line, the line of life.

The descendants of Cain and Seth are on these two separate lines. The lineage from Seth to Noah is a lineage according to the line of life. But by the time of the building of the tower of Babel, it seems the whole earth had forsaken the line of life (Gen. 11:1–9). Eventually God called out Abraham. Out of Abraham's descendants, there were also two lines. One line was Ishmael, and the other was Isaac. Isaac was on the line of life. Ishmael and Isaac struggled against one another (21:9–10). Then, from Isaac there were two lines. One line was Esau, and the other was Jacob. Jacob was on the line of life. These two brothers also struggled against each other even in the womb (25:22–23). The entire history of the human race is a history of the struggle between these two lines. Mankind is always struggling because God has placed two lines on the earth, and every human being must choose between them.

We must ask ourselves, "Am I in the line of life, or am I in the line of the knowledge of good and evil?" If we are in the line of life, then we are living according to what God desires. If we are living in the line of knowledge, living according to even our good logic, then we are living in the improper line rejected by God.

Cain—Acquisition

After the fall of man, the physical world changed drastically. Formerly, the sun was pleasant, but now the sun caused people to sweat. Formerly, no animal was harmful, but now animals became dangerous. Adam and Eve experienced many drastic changes, and they knew that it was because of the serpent's temptation. They must have hated that serpent far beyond our understanding.

But God had said that the seed of the woman would bruise the serpent's head (Gen. 3:15). When Adam and Eve finally had a son, they called his name Cain, which means "acquisition; possession" (Potts, p. 60). This name indicates that once they acquired Cain, they believed they had gained the seed of the woman God had promised.

Adam and Eve must have been joyful, thinking that this son was going to bruise the serpent's head. They may even have hoped that after the head of the serpent was bruised, everything on earth would be restored back to its original state. They would no longer need to work so hard and sweat for food. The curse would be over, and things would be just as they had been before the fall. They waited for Cain to grow up to fulfill God's promise, but the more he grew, the more disappointed they must have become, realizing that he could not possibly be the one to bruise the serpent's head.

Abel—Vanity

When Adam and Eve's second son was born, they named him Abel, which means "vanity; transitoriness" (Potts, p. 14). By naming their second son Abel, they were saying, "It's all vanity. This son won't work either. God will never crush the serpent's head and restore the earth by using either of our two boys. It is all hopeless." If neither of their sons would bruise the serpent's head, then what had happened to God's promise? Their hope of seeing creation restored to its former beautiful and restful condition was dashed. God's beautiful creation had been ruined by eating one small fruit from the wrong tree. Adam and Eve must have longed to go back to what they had in the beginning. The first son didn't bruise the serpent's head, so by the time the second son was born, they realized how hopeless their situation was. After the disappointment of Cain, they concluded that their fallen existence was futile, empty, and meaningless. This is why they named their second son Abel.

The birth of Cain was a time of excitement and expectation. The birth of Abel was a time of disappointment and vanity. Cain signifies, "I got it!" Abel signifies, "It's all useless!" These two names are very meaningful. Cain and Abel, acquisition and vanity, represent the two manners of life. They are the beginning of the two lines, the line of knowledge and the line of life. Cain's line began with assurance. Abel's line began with disappointment. The line of knowledge began with "I got it." The line of life began with "I don't have it." The two manners of life are characterized by these two names.

Regulated by Revelation

Both Cain and Abel heard from their parents that after the fall, God told them to labor on the land for food and then clothed them with animal skins. Cain only had an objective understanding: "God said we should labor on the land, so I will be a farmer. I must live according to God's commandment." But Abel had a revelation: "God clothed them with skins, so I must be a shepherd. I must live according to God's provision for my salvation."

Cain was regulated by his understanding of God's commandment, but Abel was regulated by his revelation based on God's provision. The significant difference between them was that Cain could eat of the fruit of his own labor, but Abel could not. At this point in human history, people were not yet eating meat, so the flock that Abel tended was not used for food. Abel must have depended on what his brother Cain produced by laboring in the field. Cain's life was one of outward success and productivity. With Abel's life, however, there was no glory.

With almost everything we do in our human life, there are tangible results. Those who enjoy writing can work hard and eventually become journalists. Those who enjoy music can practice faithfully and become musicians. If we work hard at anything, eventually we will have something to show for it, but when we love the Lord, there is nothing to show for it. There is no trophy, no visible gain. If we want to follow the Lord, we should be very clear about this. We must realize that if we follow the Lord, we will be misunderstood and unappreciated. Everyone else may have something to show for how they live, but our lives will be different if we live according to revelation.

This was the life of Abel—a life of seeming vanity. It was a life of revelation, not outward success. When we live according to a revelation of Christ, we must realize that such a life will not be appreciated by others. They will feel that that our life is meaningless. Concerning himself and those who served with him, Paul testified, "We have become as the scum of the world, the dregs of all things" (1 Cor. 4:13). Abel's life seemed empty and vain. If we are in the line of Abel, we will be able to say, "I only desire God. I have nothing else but God Himself. I'm not in the line of Cain who labored to acquire. People may think my life is meaningless because for me, everything apart from God is vain."

How do we see this vision and live in the line of Abel? The key is our human spirit. Whenever we touch our spirit, the vision of the Lord is there. Paul prayed that God would give the Ephesian believers "a spirit of wisdom and of revelation in the knowledge of Him" (Eph. 1:17). A person in spirit is a person with vision. When we touch our spirit, we see something, just as Abel saw something from the sharing of his father. We may wonder about our future. On Abel's line, we have no future. If we realize that our name is "vanity," then we have nothing more to gain on this earth. Our life will only be for Jesus Christ. He is all that we desire. Our life will then be regulated by our vision of the Lord and His salvation.

Abel's Testimony of God's Salvation

Abel saw a vision concerning God's provision for salvation and then lived according to that vision. He became a shepherd, not a farmer. He knew that without the shedding of blood, signifying a Savior who would die for him, he could not see the face of God. This is why Abel needed to offer of the firstlings of his flock. God had regard to Abel's offering and rejected Cain's because Abel's offering typifies the need for a Savior and the offering up of Christ. Abel realized his need for the shedding of blood in order to come into God's presence. Abel never knew the Lord Jesus directly or that He would die for mankind's salvation, but he did realize that only by the shedding of blood could he come to God. This was God's provision for his salvation.

Cain's Murdering of His Brother

Cain's life was regulated by his understanding of the need to keep God's commandment. He wanted to do something to make God happy. What better way than to do what God told him to do? But God didn't even regard Cain's offering. The result of Cain's trying to please God by keeping His commandment was that he eventually murdered his brother. Cain may have slain Abel in the very field where he labored on the land in obedience to God's commandment (Gen. 4:10–12). It is even possible that Cain murdered his brother with the tool he used to till the earth.

Why did Cain become so angry? Cain's stand was to try to please God by keeping His command, but Abel's stand was to live his life based on the salvation God had prepared for them. Abel's offering was accepted and Cain's was rejected. This is the reason that Cain was angry enough to kill Abel.

Seth—Appointed by God

After Abel was murdered, God gave Adam and Eve another son. Eve named him Seth, saying, "God has appointed me another offspring in place of Abel" (Gen. 4:25). After Abel's death, God appointed Seth to carry out His purpose. Without the death of Abel, there could not be the appointing of Seth. Seth was the continuation of Abel. These two are as one person in the line of life. However, there was a process involved. Abel lived a regulated life based on a firm stand according to a vision of the sacrifice and salvation that God had prepared. Abel's life, a life of seeming vanity, ended in his premature death. But after Abel's death, God brought him into resurrection through Seth, the appointed one. In the principle of resurrection, Seth was appointed to carry out God's purpose.

Living by Vision

In following the Lord, we should never forget these two manners of life. We must avoid the line of Cain, which is the line of the knowledge of good and evil. We should not live by regulations and commands or by our religious understanding. We must live in the line of Abel, the line of life and revelation. We should tell the Lord, "My life on this earth seems vain and empty. There is nothing for me to gain here except You. I must have You alone. You are my Savior and my salvation. I want my life to be regulated according to the vision You have shown me. Even if my life is misunderstood by others, I know it is appreciated by You." What a consecration this is!

The vision we see regulates our lives. Abel's living was regulated according to his vision of God's salvation. As a shepherd, his offering was a picture of Christ. It was a testimony of his realization that he needed God's salvation. Eventually, Abel's regulated living led to his physical death at the hand of his brother. But through his death, Abel figuratively experienced resurrection. This resurrection was an appointing, as seen in Seth. This was the glorious result of Abel's regulated living according to his vision. This must become our experience on the line of life.

3

Cain and
His Descendants

Two Lines and Two Realms

Cain and Abel were not the only descendants of Adam and Eve. They had more sons and daughters after these two (Gen. 5:4). However, Cain and Abel stand out from the other descendants because they represent the two manners of life. One manner of life begins with acquisition, and the other begins with vanity. From Cain and Abel, two lines on this earth developed, and two different realms were produced. The first realm, from the line of Cain, is of the satanic domain of darkness. The second realm, from the line of Abel, is the kingdom of God's beloved Son (Col. 1:13). These two realms are always struggling and fighting against each other.

Cain and Abel both learned the story of the fall of man from their parents, yet their reactions were very different. Cain only heard God's commandment to live by laboring on the land. Abel saw a vision of depending on God for salvation, as signified by the garments of skin God prepared for his parents. Cain lived according to what he heard, while Abel lived according to what he saw. In our Christian life, we may have heard many things, but until we see them in our spirit, they are not really ours. They are not yet our vision. Our life should be affected not merely by the things we have heard but even more by the things we see in our spirit. When we live according to what we see in our spirit, we are living in the line of life.

Cain Loses God's Presence

After Cain murdered Abel, God came to him and asked, "Where is Abel your brother?" Cain responded, "I do not know. Am I my brother's keeper?" (Gen. 4:9). Cain, who had tried to do everything according to his understanding of God's commandment, became so cruel and evil. Then God said, "What have you done? The voice of your brother's blood is crying to Me from the ground. Now you are cursed from the ground, which has opened its mouth to receive your brother's blood from your hand" (vv. 10–11). Even the earth itself had sympathy for Abel. God judged Cain by strengthening the curse on the ground and driving Cain away from His presence: "When you cultivate the ground, it will no longer yield its strength to you; you will be a vagrant and a wanderer on the earth" (v. 12). Cain's reaction was, "My punishment is too great to bear! Behold, You have driven me this day from the face of the ground; and from Your face I will be hidden, and I will be a vagrant and a wanderer on the earth, and whoever finds me will kill me" (vv. 13–14). From that time, Cain lost God's presence. He became a vagrant and a wanderer. This caused him to fear for his life.

Cain was a typical human being in that he was so complicated. Part of him sought to please God, but part of him was a murderer. Ever since his father first told him about God's command to cultivate the ground, Cain did his best to keep that commandment according to his own understanding. When God said that he would be a vagrant and a wanderer, Cain responded, "If I don't have You I can't survive. Without You, without Your presence, without Your protection, I will be killed." This shows that Cain was not so simple. He was afraid that whoever found him would kill him because he had lost God's presence and protection. God heard and answered Cain's plea, saying, "Therefore whoever kills Cain, vengeance will be taken on him sevenfold" (v. 15). God put a mark on him for his protection, and Cain was sent away from God's presence.

Wandering in the Land of Nod

After God put a mark on Cain and sent him away, Cain began his life of wandering. "Then Cain went out from the presence of the Lord, and settled in the land of Nod, east of Eden" (Gen. 4:16). The name "Nod" means "wandering; fugitive" (Potts, p. 185). After leaving God's presence, Cain began to wander. This can be true of us as well. Whenever we leave God's presence, regardless of what we do, we are wandering. This is a basic principle of the Christian life. For example, if we don't have God's presence while we are going to school, in God's view, we are wandering. If we are saving money for our retirement without God's presence, we are wandering. Without God, everything we do in life is wandering. This is the line of Cain. He left God's presence and ended up in the land of Nod, the land of wandering.

Enoch and Irad

The line of Cain continued with his descendants. Cain begot Enoch, whose name means "instructed" (Potts, p. 83), and Enoch begot Irad, whose name means "fleet" (Smith, p. 266), that is, fast. Learning spiritual things on the line of life is very difficult, but learning non-spiritual things on the line of knowledge is much faster. Cain's name implies gaining, Enoch's name implies learning, and Irad implies speed. Things on the line of knowledge can be gained and learned very quickly. Things on the line of life, however, take much more time to learn. The learning of worldly things is comparatively rapid, but the learning of spiritual things comes through years of pursuit.

For example, how well do we really know how to preach the gospel and shepherd new believers? How well do we know how to build up the church? Though the things of the world can be learned rapidly, spiritual things such as these take time to learn. If we were learning from Cain's line, we would have gained many PhD's already. But when we are learning to follow and serve the Lord, even after forty years, there will be no degree waiting for us. We will still be learning. Whenever we hastily decide, "Now I'm clear—now I'm going to do this," we need to be careful, for we may be acting in the line of Cain.

The learning on the line of knowledge is very productive. Cain built a city and named it after his son Enoch (Gen. 4:17). This means that a city came out of Enoch, out of the learning on the line of knowledge. It is God's ultimate intention to have a holy city, the New Jerusalem (Rev. 21:2). However, the first city in the Bible was not built by God's people but by Cain, the one God sent away from His presence. Cain's line is very productive, and everything on Cain's line moves quickly.

Mehujael

The next person in Cain's line was Mehujael, the son of Irad. Mehujael's name means "God is combating" (Potts, p. 166), indicating that God was struggling with the people in this line. God's heart for the people was to warn them that if they kept going so fast, they would ruin themselves and be hurt. They should slow down. God was fighting to rescue humanity, even those in the line of Cain.

We sometimes get caught by religious things and become extremely zealous. Zeal can be a good thing (John 2:17), but it can also be in the principle of the line of Cain (Gal. 4:17). If we think that doing a certain thing zealously means we are spiritual, we are on the wrong line. The things on the line of life never come that quickly or easily. When we go too fast, God enters into combat, fighting for us to return to the line of life.

Methusael

Mehujael had a son named Methusael, which means "man of God" (Potts, p. 171). How can there be a man of God on the line of Cain? God's combating seemingly produced a man of God in the wrong line. However, we must see that Cain's descendants never departed from the line of knowledge, which belongs to the satanic realm. Satan, God's enemy, was still the ruler of this line, even with Methusael, the man of God. We know this because eventually Methusael begot Lamech, a boastful murderer. Even with God's combating, producing a man of God, this line was still under the ruling of Satan.

Lamech

Next in the line of Cain's descendants was Lamech, whose name means "powerful; wild man" (Potts, p. 153). He was a wild and evil man, a true representative of Cain's line. Lamech murdered a man and then boasted to his wives, "I have killed a man for wounding me; and a boy for striking me; if Cain is avenged sevenfold, then Lamech seventy-sevenfold" (Gen. 4:23–24). This is the result of the line of Cain. It is shocking that out of Cain, who had such a strong desire to keep God's commandment, came descendants who could fall this low. This should be a strong warning to us all. Cain and Abel believed in the same God, but one was in the line of knowledge and one was in the line of life. After Cain murdered Abel, his descendants became even worse. Lamech was not only a murderer but was proud and even boastful of it. He represents the ultimate manifestation of evil on the line of knowledge.

Good Becoming Evil

Cain's original desire to keep God's commandment was good. Good and evil are not necessarily opposites. Anything good from the line of knowledge can eventually become evil. Many things that begin right can end up very wrong. Throughout church history, those who have persecuted the Lord's people the most have been the religious ones, those who try to keep God's commandments, yet without life. They have ended up persecuting and even killing those who follow the Lord on the line of life. The original desire of religious people may be good, but the outcome can be so evil. This is what happened with Cain and his descendants. Eventually Lamech represented the ultimate manifestation of evil from the line of knowledge.

Cain wanted to keep God's commandment, but eventually he became a murderer and went out from God's presence. However, God still protected him, telling him, "Whoever kills Cain, vengeance will be taken on him sevenfold" (Gen. 4:15). Eventually, Cain's descendant Lamech also became a murderer. Afterward, he neither repented nor asked the Lord for mercy but instead boasted to his wives. The line of Cain, which began with Cain's desire to keep God's commandment, ended up with Lamech boasting in murder. On the line of knowledge, something good easily becomes evil.

We should pray, "Lord, have mercy on me. I don't want to live by my knowledge of what is good and what is evil. I don't want to live by my logic, by what seems reasonable, or by what others think is proper. I realize that apart from You, any good thing can become evil. Lord, only You can save me. I want to live by You. Please keep me in the line of life."

Jabal, Jubal, and Tubal-cain

In Genesis 4, the line of Cain ends with Lamech and his three sons. The main pillars of human civilization developed from Lamech's descendants. Lamech's first son was Jabal, "the father of those who dwell in tents and have livestock" (Gen. 4:20). Jabal's life was for making a living. Lamech's second son was Jubal, "the father of all those who play the lyre and pipe" (v. 21). He was a musician, and his life was for entertainment. Lamech's third son was Tubal-cain, "the forger of all implements of bronze and iron" (v. 22). His work would have included forging weapons. These are the three sons of Lamech.

Jabal signifies making a living, Jubal signifies making our lives enjoyable, and Tubal-cain signifies defending ourselves and attacking others. These three things are the three main pillars of human civilization. Whatever we study, gain, or pursue in the world eventually brings us to one of these three sons of Lamech, for they are the source of all human culture and society.

This is significant, because Lamech was a murderer. When the human race is without God, it is a killing race. Human history is just a history of killing. In principle, this is true throughout society. In universities, businesses, and professions, people are all competing. People think, "For me to survive, you must die." They "kill" one another to get ahead and even boast in their success. This is because human culture is the product of the line of Cain.

Satan's Control of Human Society

Human culture and society are completely controlled by Satan. No human being can escape. Either we are making a living, enjoying entertainment, or attacking and defending. Whatever we do in our human life, Satan corners us into one of these three things. We cannot escape this. "The whole world lies in the power of the evil one" (1 John 5:19). Through the line of Cain with the three sons of Lamech, the evil one has control over every God-created human being. Satan controls the human race by our struggle for our living, our entertainment, and our defense. This is the manifestation of the line of Cain.

God's Use of Fallen Civilization

Even though human civilization is from the line of knowledge, God is still able to use it. For example, God uses human inventions. Under Satan's control, man has invented many things, such as new methods of communication and new computer technology. God uses these inventions for Himself. God's people on the line of life use these inventions from the line of knowledge for the furthering of God's purpose.

This principle is also true on a greater scale. The first city in the Bible was Enoch, built by Cain, but the last city in the Bible is the New Jerusalem. Even today, in so many cities which man has built and which Satan controls, God has His churches, His golden lampstands (Rev. 1:11–12, 20). In the cities of Satan, there are the churches of God. Eventually these churches make up one city, the New Jerusalem.

We have to admire God's wisdom. Satan may control all of human society through the line of Cain, but God still has a way to work with man through the line of life. Those who are on the line of life can use what has been produced by those on the line of knowledge for the fulfillment of God's purpose.

A Return to the Line of Life

Even though Satan has control over human society, and even though his kingdom seems so prevailing, God is still doing something hidden through those on the line of life.

Everything Satan does through those on the line of knowledge is clearly manifested, but what God does through those on the line of life is not always outwardly visible. Even though it may be hidden, it is precious in God's sight.

At the end of Genesis 4, after recording all the descendants of Cain, the Bible returns to the line of life: "Adam had relations with his wife again; and she gave birth to a son, and named him Seth, for, she said, 'God has appointed me another offspring in place of Abel, for Cain killed him.' To Seth, to him also a son was born; and he called his name Enosh. Then men began to call upon the name of the Lord" (Gen. 4:25–26). The next chapter of Genesis is a new beginning on the line of life.

4

A New Beginning

After all of the negative things in Genesis 4, we need a new beginning. Genesis 5 is a fresh new beginning on the line of life: "This is the book of the generations of Adam. In the day when God created man, He made him in the likeness of God" (Gen. 5:1). In this verse, it seems that God ignored everything that happened in the previous chapter. In Genesis 4, Cain murdered Abel. Then Cain's line continued with all of his descendants. Eventually the line of Cain resulted in the totality of human culture and society through the three sons of Lamech. Genesis 4 is only positive at the end: "Then men began to call upon the name of the Lord" (Gen. 4:26).

Chapter 5 continues, "He created them male and female, and He blessed them and named them Man in the day when they were created" (v. 2). These verses sound almost exactly the same as Genesis 1. In Genesis 5, God has a new beginning. There is no more Cain and no more Abel. In the sight of God, there is only Seth, the appointed one (4:25). All the negative and unpleasant things from chapter 4 have disappeared. Now there is a new beginning according to the line of life. This is what we experience when we follow the Lord. With the Lord, in His presence, there is always a new beginning. This is a wonderful and comforting realization.

God's Deleting Ability

Genesis 5:3 tells us, "When Adam had lived one hundred and thirty years, he became the father of a son in his own likeness, according to his image, and named him Seth." Cain and Abel were both gone. It was as if they never existed. This chapter simply tells us that Adam lived one hundred thirty years and became the father of Seth. It states this as if Seth were his first son. Everything that happened in chapter 4 disappeared. This shows us that God has a great deleting ability. In chapter 5, God deleted all the negative things that were in chapter 4 and simply started over.

How are we able to survive in our Christian life? Why can we still tell the Lord, "I love You"? It is because God has a great deleting ability. If God couldn't delete, it would be very serious for us. We would all be in trouble.

The Counting of Years

In Genesis 5, the age of each of those included on the line of life is recorded. For example, Adam lived a total of nine hundred thirty years (v. 5). This is in contrast to those in the line of knowledge in chapter 4. Their years did not count to God and were not recorded. He didn't care how many years they lived. God may use their inventions for His purpose, but He doesn't count their age. Adam's age, however, was counted. The Bible records that at the age of one hundred thirty, Adam begot Seth. Then after he begot Seth he lived eight hundred more years for a total of nine hundred thirty years (vv. 3–5). On the line of life, everyone's years are counted.

People may live for many years, but if those years are on the line of knowledge, in God's eyes they are not counted. He only counts the years that are on the line of life. The age of those who live in the principle of the line of Cain and his descendants is actually zero according to God's accounting. If we were to ask those who are great in the world, "How old are you?" many would have to answer, "According to God's accounting, I'm only zero years old." We don't know how long those in the line of Cain lived because their lives had no value in the sight of God. But the lives of those on the line of life have value. God specifically and deliberately counts their years. He cares how old they became.

God only counts the years in which we live in the line of life. In these many years we live on this earth, even after we are saved, how much have we lived in the line of life? The years we spend in the line of life are the only years that truly count in the sight of God.

Seth—Appointed

After the death of Abel, the line of life continued with Adam's son Seth: "Adam had relations with his wife again; and she gave birth to a son, and named him Seth, for, she said, 'God has appointed me another offspring in place of Abel, for Cain killed him'" (Gen. 4:25). Seth followed the martyred Abel, just as the resurrected Christ follows the crucified Christ. Seth was appointed by God, and we also are appointed, having been chosen before the foundation of the world (Eph. 1:4). Just as Seth came out of the death of Abel, we were regenerated through the resurrection of Jesus Christ from the dead (1 Pet. 1:3) and transferred to a completely new realm, the kingdom of God's beloved Son (Col. 1:13). In this divine and mystical realm, we began to experience the life supply that we need for going through all the stages of our Christian life. Seth does not represent a stage of our Christian life but the divine and mystical realm, in which we experience all of the stages on the line of life from Enosh to Noah. Now we are one with the resurrected and ascended Christ. This is the experience of Seth.

Enosh—Mortal

Seth then begot a son named Enosh, which means "a miserable man; a mortal" (Potts, p. 83). Seth was the appointed one, yet he named his son "mortal." For Seth to name his son Enosh was to say, "I know I am the appointed one, but I also know that I am weak and mortal. I know that my descendants and I will die."

After we are appointed (Seth) and enter the kingdom of God's Son, the first stage of our Christian life is to realize that we are mortal (Enosh). This begins at our regeneration when we repent and turn to the Lord. Because we realize that we are weak and mortal, we turn to the Lord and receive another life. Everything we are by nature does not count. Once we are saved, we must learn how to live by the life we received at regeneration.

Unfortunately, most Christians join themselves to the line of the knowledge of good and evil after experiencing the appointment of Seth through their regeneration. Very few realize that to continue living the Christian life after their regeneration, they must learn that they are weak and mortal, needing the Lord's mercy. This is to grow from Seth to Enosh in our experience. Those who realize that they are appointed should also sense that they are mortal. Since we have been appointed by God, we may think we should feel glorious. But when we genuinely grow in the Lord, we realize that we are weak, mortal, and limited. We have so little. This is the significance of Enosh.

After we realize that we are mortal, what should we do? The Bible tells us that after the birth of Enosh, "men began to call upon the name of the Lord" (Gen. 4:26). We call on Him because, even though we are in the line of life, we are still mortal. One of the Lord's greatest blessings is to show us our true condition—fragile, mortal, and weak. Once we see this, we can only call upon Him. To call on the Lord means that we know we desperately need Him. We realize that we cannot possibly go on without Him.

When we know that we are mortal (Enosh), we are able to grow, and the more we grow, the more we realize we are mortal. Instead of growing stronger, it seems that we grow weaker and more limited. Previously, we felt we could subdue everyone, but now it seems that everyone else subdues us. The more we grow in the line of life, the more we realize our weakness and mortality. Everything we gain spiritually must come from the realization that we are Enosh. Only then can we truly follow the Lord and be used by Him.

In the line of the knowledge of good and evil, there was a man with a good desire who tried to keep God's commandment. This man, Cain, produced a line of descendants. Eventually, Cain's line resulted in Lamech, a man who was strong and boastful, who felt that no man was his equal. He was the totality of the evil nature in fallen man. But in the line of life, there was another man, Abel, who saw a vision and lived according to that vision. Through Seth, the line of Abel produced Enosh. Because Enosh knew he was weak and mortal, he called on the Lord's name. We are all proud by nature and think we are somebody. But the more we realize how weak we are, the more we will call on the Lord. The more we call, the more the Lord is with us in our experience. This is to experience Enosh in the line of life.

5

Mortality Leading to Possession

When we began to love the Lord, we felt so powerful, strong, buoyant, and confident. This was because we had the experience of Seth, the appointed one. For us to feel this way was proper at the beginning of our Christian life. Furthermore, when we first loved the Lord, we were filled with life and enjoyment. We felt so close to Him. This is the experience of Seth, the beginning of our experience in the line of life.

However, we may start to consider ourselves spiritually mature. We may even think we are ready to be great spiritual workers. Once we feel that we are somebody, the Lord will begin to show us who we really are. He will seem to withdraw His upholding and protecting power. Formerly, we felt so powerful and strong, but when He moves His hand just a little, we cry out, "Oh Lord Jesus, I need You!" This is our experience of Enosh.

Kenan—A Possessor

Enosh's son was named Kenan (Gen. 5:9) or Cainan (KJV). This name is very similar to Cain. "Cain" means "acquisition," and "Kenan" means "a possessor" (Potts, p. 60). With both the line of life and the line of knowledge, there is something to acquire and possess.

The gaining of spiritual things is very different from the gaining of worldly things. Everything in this world is readily acquired. The principle of the line of knowledge is that those who apply themselves will gain what they are after. Furthermore, once they gain it, they become very proud and self-assured. As those who follow the Lord, we must live by a different principle. The Lord doesn't want to make us proud or self-assured. The more we know how weak we really are, the more we are able to apprehend spiritual things. It is foolish for us to boast that we have already obtained (Phil. 3:12). No matter how much we see, or how much we have gained, it cannot possibly compare with "the unfathomable riches of Christ" (Eph. 3:8). The only way we can possess these riches is by confessing that we are weak and mortal. This is how Enosh begets Kenan in our experience. Out of the realization of our weakness, we gain Christ.

The realization of our weaknesses and the gaining of Christ happen almost simultaneously. The more we realize that we are Enosh, the more we become Kenan. One is just a step ahead of the other. This is a process we never outgrow. Though we may be so aware of our weaknesses, others realize that we have gained Christ. While we say, "I'm defeated," others will say, "You've grown." The experiences of Enosh and Kenan go together.

Spiritual gain is not according to our religious thought. When young believers shout, "Praise the Lord! I have overcome!" it is difficult to trust this declaration. But suppose instead they repent with tears, praying, "Lord, I'm so poor. I'm so weak and limited. I don't even know why You still love me and have mercy on me." This is the prayer of Christians who are growing. They are experiencing Enosh on the line of life. Out of this realization of their weakness, they will enter into the experience of Kenan. By realizing their mortality and by desperately seeking and calling on the Lord, they will gain the spiritual riches on the line of life.

Experiencing Weakness to
Gain Spiritual Possessions

The Lord wants us to realize that we are Enosh—weak and mortal. For example, He may allow our temper to grow worse. Even while we pray to overcome, we continue to lose our temper. Our feeling is, "Lord, how can I love You so much yet lose my temper so often?" But the Lord doesn't do anything about our temper until we learn that we are Enosh. He can't afford to free us from our temper because we would think we are somebody again. Even the apostle Paul was given a thorn in the flesh to keep him from exalting himself (2 Cor. 12:7). Our realization of our weakness causes us to call on the Lord (Gen. 4:26). Eventually, we become Kenan. We may struggle against our temper until we finally tell the Lord, "I can't make it. I'm just too weak." In this process, eventually we will gain something. The Lord may give us a revelation, showing us that we died with Christ. Since a dead person has no temper, we don't need to be freed from it. When He shows us this, it becomes our spiritual possession. We have entered into the experience of Kenan, the possessor.

We can only experience Kenan after realizing we are Enosh. As we grow in the line of life, God lets us experience our weaknesses. It may be our temper, our looseness, or our love for something other than the Lord. We should not feel too discouraged, defeated, or overly bothered by them. Rather, we should cry out to the Lord in the midst of our weakness. That is to be Enosh. We can simply cry out, "Lord, I need You!" Our weaknesses are actually for our spiritual gain. When we realize how limited and fragile we are, our prayer becomes different. We spend more time praying for the Lord's mercy and less time feeling good about our successes. Enosh begets Kenan in our experience, for we have gained genuine spiritual possessions.

Knowledge Becoming Experience

Our spiritual learning on the line of life must be experiential. The process of our growth is not merely one of knowing or learning but of possessing. We must possess spiritual things subjectively. We may think that as long as we know something, we have it. This is wrong. If we only have the knowledge of something without the spiritual experience, it is not sufficient. Yes, we do need to know many things for our Christian life. In fact, the more we know the better, because without proper knowledge, our experience will be limited. But we should never think that what we know is what we truly possess.

Spiritual Things Taking Time

We have previously seen that in the line of Cain, things go very quickly. Cain begot Enoch and built a city in Enoch's name. Enoch had a son named Irad, which means fleet or fast. Eventually from Cain's descendants, human culture developed in three aspects. But in the spiritual life, on the line of life, things do not go so quickly. For example, how many years did those in Genesis 5 have to live before they begot a son who was counted? Sometimes it was more than a hundred years. Why did those on the line of life beget children at such an old age? It is possible that they had other children before those recorded in the Bible. In the sight of God, they were not counted. In each case, when someone on the line of life finally had enough experience to give birth to a son who counted, the child's name was recorded in the Bible, for this one was in the line of life.

Spiritual things do not come quickly. They do not come through what we call victory. The real spiritual things are gained over a long period of time as we recognize our weaknesses and fragility. It takes a long time for us to realize who we are and how much we need the Lord. In that time, we may produce many things that are not counted by Him. Eventually, we realize that we are mortal. When we turn to the Lord and call on Him out of our desperation, we can gain real spiritual things.

Using Our Time to Gain Spiritual Riches

"Enosh" refers to human weakness and mortality. The realization of our mortality should cause us to live differently. Our time on this earth is only temporary. How much we acquire and gain spiritually is based on how we handle our limited time. Even if we have heard many high, profound teachings, the reality of them may not yet be ours. We need them to become our subjective experience. We must desire and pursue the spiritual riches until they are ours experientially. God has given many rich truths to us, but we must realize that we are mortal and our time is limited. We must treasure our time and use it to gain spiritual riches. We should never relax but fully utilize the time God has given us. This is to use our mortal life (Enosh) to possess spiritual riches (Kenan).

It is easy to have such an understanding, but it is not as easy for this understanding to regulate our life. To become possessors of genuine spiritual riches, we must realize that we are mortal and our time is valuable. We should pray, "Lord, I want to treasure everything You have given me—all the time, talent, and capacity in this mortal life. I want to invest it all in You so that I can become a possessor of spiritual riches."

Our desire is to grow from Enosh to Kenan. How do we become Kenan, that is, how do we become possessors of spiritual riches? We gain them as we understand our weaknesses and limitations. If we can't see our weaknesses, we are not yet Enosh and do not have the experience of Kenan. If we think that we are strong and powerful, our growth in life will be hindered. We learn the real spiritual things when we know how fragile we are. This is especially true when we serve the Lord. We should tell the Lord, "If I can do anything for You, it is by Your mercy. If I can help one person to be saved, if I can help one person to grow, if I can serve the church in any way, it is all by Your mercy. I am so mortal. I am just weak, fragile, and limited. Lord, all I can do is call on You." Once we realize we are mortal, we are ready to become possessors of the spiritual things on the line of life.

6

Praising and Descending

When we first believed in the Lord, we were appointed and transferred into the realm of Seth, the kingdom of God's beloved Son. In this realm, the experience of Christ is all-inclusive—it includes Enosh, Kenan, and all the other names on the line of life. In this realm, we grow in life. When we are exposed concerning our weaknesses, that is the time we gain Christ. While God is reminding us that we are Enosh, He is simultaneously revealing Christ to us so that we can be Kenan. This is the process of growth in the Christian life. It is not just for our understanding but for our experience.

Mahalalel—Praising God

The next person on the line of life is Kenan's son Mahalalel (Gen. 5:12), which means "praising God" (Potts, p. 160). This is a very significant progression. First, we experience being weak and mortal (Enosh). Next, we become possessors of the spiritual riches of Christ (Kenan). Then, we begin to praise God (Mahalalel). Whenever we gain something of God, we completely forget about ourselves and spontaneously begin to praise Him. Our appreciation of God becomes different: He is above everything; He is more honorable and more glorious than everything. Do we have such a God, or is our God small?

When we have the experience of Mahalalel, we praise God because we realize how grand He is.

Unfortunately, our attitude may be, "God is marvelous, and so am I!" Whenever we think we are so good, God humbles us. He may even allow us to fall into the world for a period of time. Eventually, we come back to Him and say, "Lord, forgive me. I am nothing. I need Your mercy." Since we are so fragile, we fear leaving the Lord's presence. This healthy realization will cause us to grow. When we realize our limitation and mortality, we will be so dependent on Him, never wanting to leave Him. When we experience this, it becomes our stability.

The experience of Enosh will lead us to the experience of Kenan. Only after we realize that we are so limited will we gain more and more of the riches of Christ. On one hand, we feel that we are so mortal, even to the point of being utterly helpless. But on the other hand, the Lord is adding Himself to us, causing us to grow in Him. This is an organic process. Then, as we gain the Lord, we also realize, "God, You are the only One worthy of praise! You are magnificent!" This is Mahalalel. Now we know who we are, and we know who God is. We know that only God is praiseworthy.

Growth in the line of life is much slower and harder than in the line of knowledge. Cain begot Enoch and built a city. Enoch begot Irad (fleet or fast). A few generations later, the three main pillars of human culture were produced from Cain's descendants. Everything on the line of Cain happens quickly, but in the line of life, growth is slower and harder. In Enosh, we realize our mortality and weakness. In Kenan, we experience and gain something of God. In Mahalalel, we become praisers of God. The process we go through on the line of life is difficult and takes time.

A Deeper Praise

The deeper and richer praise to God only comes as we

gain the spiritual riches of Christ. Without this, our praise will be shallow. For example, suppose a young man likes a young woman. He is afraid that if he calls her, she will reject him, so he prays to the Lord out of his anxiety. Then he calls her up. To his surprise, she is happy to go out with him. In his excitement, he offers praise to God, saying, "Thank You, God! You're wonderful!" But this is not the deeper and richer praise of Mahalalel, which only comes out of the experience of Enosh and Kenan.

However, suppose a young man has a girlfriend before he is saved. They genuinely love one another. Eventually, the young man believes in the Lord. His girlfriend makes an effort to go along with him because she loves him, but since she is not willing to become a Christian, continuing with him becomes too difficult for her. She ends the relationship. This creates a deep wound in his heart. Such a suffering is almost unbearable. He feels so tremendously sorrowful that he thinks it is better to die than to live without his loved one. He is experiencing the weakness and mortality of Enosh.

Then, suppose this young man begins to touch the Lord in the midst of his deep sorrow. He is brought into the Lord's presence, and his spiritual life is renewed. The Lord enters into his situation and seems more real to him than ever before. He enjoys Christ and gradually comes out of his suffering. After having gained Christ in this way, he prays, "Lord, thank You. This situation was much too hard for me, but I still thank You. Through this, I now know You so much more. I've experienced and enjoyed You more than ever before. Formerly, You were not so real to me, but now I know You are real. Praise You!" Out of his experience of weakness and mortality, and out of his experience of gaining Christ, he becomes a praiser of God. Eventually he can say, "Praise God! He is marvelous and full of splendor! God is worthy to be praised!" After experiencing Enosh and Kenan, he is brought to Mahalalel. None of this is merely doctrinal. We should experience this progression as we follow the Lord in the line of life.

Jared—Descent

After experiencing Mahalalel and being brought to the richer praise of God, we need the next person on the line of life. Mahalalel gave birth to Jared (Gen. 5:15), which means "descended; descent" (Potts, p. 129). There is a danger that we may experience Mahalalel to such an extreme that we become spiritually peculiar. We may become seemingly spiritual and ascend too high. The Lord wants us to be human, but instead we can become "spiritual" beings. We may become so "spiritual" that no one can fellowship with us. Others may even feel that something is wrong with them because we are so "spiritual" and they are not. Weak Christians may remain weak because all around them are Mahalalels, and no one is willing to descend and be normal.

Those who refuse to descend often become very judgmental. They judge everyone unconsciously. Their very presence becomes a pressure to those around them. The Lord wants us to experience Mahalalel, but not to the point of losing our humanity. After we become a praiser of God, it is essential for us to experience Jared and learn to descend.

Many times, when we have gained even a little spiritual stature, we become different. We may feel no one loves the Lord like we do, thinking of ourselves more highly than we ought to think (Rom. 12:3). This is when we need to be careful and learn how to descend. We should know how to treat people normally. For example, when we are with those who do not love the Lord, do they feel comfortable around us and entrust themselves to us? Suppose we tell them, "Praise God for the divine economy! Isn't it glorious to enjoy the divine and mystical realm? Oh, what an organic salvation!" They will become afraid of us. They have no idea what we are talking about. How can they be brought to love the Lord if they don't see any descending on our part? We are so far above them that we have become unapproachable. We are Mahalalel, but there is no Jared in our experience.

Jared was born of Mahalalel. After we become Kenan by gaining Christ, and after we become Mahalalel, a praiser of God, then we should also learn how to descend. This is how the apostle Paul lived. He wrote, "To the weak I became weak, that I might win the weak; I have become all things to all men, so that I may by all means save some" (1 Cor. 9:22). For us to be Jared means that to the weak, we become weak. To those who are not spiritual, we don't behave spiritually, even though we are still spiritual inwardly. When we meet unbelievers, we don't say, "Praise the Lord!" because they don't even know who the Lord is. We should know how to behave and speak normally around them. If we don't know how to descend, we will be fruitless in our Christian life. We won't know how to help anyone. We must learn how to be with all kinds of people. We must have the experience of Jared, knowing how to descend.

To descend doesn't mean that we lose our proper stand. To experience Jared doesn't mean that we do things that violate our conscience to be with someone. That is not experiencing Jared; that is sinning (Rom. 14:23). We must still maintain a healthy spiritual condition. When we are with those who are unsaved, weak, or young spiritually, we must learn to be so human and not so high. If we love and care for them, we will become very approachable for their sake. After our experience of Mahalalel, a praiser of God, we must learn to be Jared and descend.

The Lord's Descending

When the Lord Jesus was on the earth, He was the real Jared. Paul gives us the best description of the Lord's descending humanity: "Christ Jesus, who, although He existed in the form of God, did not regard equality with God a thing to be grasped, but emptied Himself, taking the form of a bond-servant, and being made in the likeness of men. Being found in appearance as a man, He humbled Himself by becoming obedient to the point of death, even death on a cross" (Phil. 2:5–8). The Lord was constantly descending. In the Gospels, the Lord Jesus was with all kinds of people. He was even called "the friend of tax collectors and sinners" (Matt. 11:19). They felt He was so lovable and approachable, yet He didn't partake of their sin or worldliness.

Descending isn't something we do but rather, who we are. If by the Lord's mercy we have some growth and genuine spiritual attainment, then we will spontaneously know how to be with people. It should be very normal. We shouldn't need to think about humbling ourselves. The Lord didn't have to stop and think about each step—becoming a man, a bondservant, then humbling Himself by dying on a cross. If He descended this way, He would have been very peculiar. Descending came to Him naturally. He was a descending person by nature. The more we grow on the line of life, the more this should become our experience. As we are growing spiritually, we are also learning to love and care for all kinds of people. We are learning to spend time with them and to be normal around them.

We as believers are being conformed to the image of the Lord Jesus, the true Jared, so that we can share in His descending humanity. This is the proper humanity God desires. Eventually, all of the riches of the triune God which we have received will be tested by this one question: do we have this proper humanity? If so, others will find us approachable, full of grace and mercy. Yet we have not given up what we gained in the previous stages. All of the triune God's divine attributes which we gained in the stages of Enosh, Kenan, and Mahalalel, are exhibited through our human virtues. This is the stage of Jared, the stage of the proper humanity.

7

Learning and Walking with God

Fast and Slow Learning

The next person on the line of life is Enoch. He had the same name as Cain's son. To understand the experience that he represents, we need to compare these two Enochs, one on the line of life and the other on the line of knowledge.

We have seen that, in human history, the line of knowledge began with Cain. After Cain murdered his brother, he was sent away from the presence of the Lord. He begot a son named Enoch, which means "instructed" (Potts, p. 83). Soon after Enoch was born, Cain built a city and named it Enoch, after his son. On the line of life, there is also a man named Enoch: "Jared lived one hundred and sixty-two years, and became the father of Enoch" (Gen. 5:18). The son of Jared on the line of life has the same name as the son of Cain on the line of knowledge.

Each of these lines has an Enoch, meaning "instructed," because there is learning on both lines. The first Enoch, Cain's son, represents the learning on the line of knowledge. He is an Enoch of doctrine. The second Enoch, Jared's son, represents the learning on the line of life. He is an Enoch of experience. The Enoch on the line of knowledge came quickly. He was the first generation after Cain. But the Enoch on the line of life came five generations after Seth. There is a process of learning signified by Enoch on both lines. However, the learning on the line of life is much harder and slower to obtain.

We should ask ourselves, "Which Enoch am I?" We like to think we have learned something, but the real spiritual learning is not so quick and easy. On the line of knowledge, the learning comes fast, but that learning is not the real learning. The real learning is the learning on the line of life, and that takes time. On the line of life, things happen very slowly. There is a long and sometimes difficult process involved in learning spiritual things.

The Slow Process of Learning

The genealogical record in Genesis 5 shows us that it takes a long time to learn on the line of life. Adam lived one hundred thirty years and then begot Seth. Seth lived one hundred five years before he begot Enosh. This description in the Bible continues with Enosh, Kenan, Mahalalel, and Jared. Each person lived many years before begetting a son who was recorded.

But on the line of Cain, there are no years mentioned. Cain begot Enoch, and then built a city. Enoch begot Irad, Irad begot Mehujael, Mehujael begot Methushael, and Methushael begot Lamech. Then Lamech begot three sons. There is just one name after another without any years being counted.

Both the line of knowledge and the line of life have an Enoch, but learning on the line of knowledge takes less time. Spiritual learning on the line of life is a slower and more difficult process. It requires paying a price.

Learning for Responsibility

The Lord Jesus said, "From everyone who has been given much, much will be required; and to whom they entrusted much, of him they will ask all the more" (Luke 12:48). What we have received from the Lord should result in our bearing responsibility before Him. An instructed person in the line of life is a responsible person. The stage of Enoch is the stage of paying a price to have the true learning with the realization that this learning is for bearing responsibility. Learning on the line of life is very demanding because it is a higher learning. It is easy to carry out spiritual activities, but to have the learning required to bear responsibility is not easy. It is the result of a process. First, the Lord must show us that we are nothing. Then, He must show us that we can gain His unfathomable riches. Then, we realize how marvelous He is and are filled with praise. After this, we descend and exhibit His humanity. Enoch represents the stage of learning on the line of life. This learning comes by paying a price. Only by paying a price can we bear responsibility on the line of life.

Real learning causes us to bear responsibility. Are we bearing responsibility related to reading and studying the Bible? Do we properly bear responsibility in serving the church? Are we bearing responsibility related to gospel preaching? Are we responsible in our praying? Are we responsible in our shepherding? If our answer to one of these questions is "no," then in that aspect of our Christian life we are not yet Enoch; we are not yet instructed. We have not paid the price to learn the spiritual things. All these aspects of our Christian life require paying a price. When our spiritual life is merely inspirational, we must still be in the earlier stages of the line of life. The earlier stages should cause us to grow until we are willing to pay the price to learn. To be Enoch is to be mature and responsible to God. When we are at the stage of Enoch, God's desire becomes our living.

Walking with God

What the Bible tells us about Enoch is very significant: "Enoch lived sixty-five years, and became the father of Methuselah. Then Enoch walked with God three hundred years after he became the father of Methuselah, and he had other sons and daughters. So all the days of Enoch were three hundred and sixty-five years. Enoch walked with God; and he was not, for God took him" (Gen. 5:21–24). Enoch only lived three hundred sixty-five years. That is the shortest life span of all the generations on the line of life in chapter 5. He lived for such a comparatively short time because he "walked with God; and he was not, for God took him."

With Enoch, we see that to walk with God is related to bearing responsibility. Because he was instructed, he bore responsibility. Since Enoch is the result of the progression on the line of life, his learning came by paying the price through the previous four generations. The result of this learning was a man who was responsible to God. The Bible doesn't tell us directly that Enoch bore responsibility before God. It simply tells us that Enoch "walked with God."

Enoch was a genuinely spiritual man. The Bible tells us twice that Enoch walked with God. This is because there are two aspects of walking with God. Verse 22 says, "Enoch walked with God…and he had other sons and daughters." Verse 24 says, "Enoch walked with God; and he was not, for God took him."

Living a Normal Life

As Enoch walked with God, he had sons and daughters. This is not the natural concept of what it is to be spiritual. We may think that those who walk with God would never have children. In other words, we think that walking with God requires escaping from the normal human life by going to some mountain or hiding ourselves in a monastery to pray all day long. But Enoch wasn't a monk. He still had a normal human life. He was married and even had sons and daughters. This shows us that to be a spiritual man is to be very normal.

Enoch was a spiritual man and thus an instructed man on the line of life. Yet his living was extremely normal—he had sons and daughters. His life was the same as that of other people. He was so normal because he had the learning of Jared, his father. He knew how to descend. Although Enoch was spiritual, he also knew how to descend. Yet in his normal, descended living, he walked with God. Some people think that they must become peculiar in order to walk with God. But those who are truly spiritual do not live abnormally. Enoch was normal. His living was the same as that of others. To be spiritual is not what we think. A spiritual person who walks with God lives a normal human life.

The only way for us to come to Enoch's generation on the line of life is through Jared. We must learn to descend and live as a normal human being. The more normal we are, the better. We don't need to be peculiar. We should not try to act differently to be spiritual. Enoch was a true spiritual man. He represents the highest spirituality, because eventually he was taken by God and was not. To walk with God is to live a normal human life. This means that those who are students should study hard. Those who have jobs should work diligently. Those who have children should care for them. Even in following and serving the Lord, we should be normal. This is the first aspect of what it means to walk with God.

"And He Was Not"

After showing us that Enoch was normal, the Bible then shows us another aspect of walking with God. "Enoch walked with God; and he was not, for God took him" (Gen. 5:24). In verse 22, Enoch walked with God and had sons and daughters, which shows that he was normal. In verse 24, Enoch walked with God and was not. He was "taken up so that he would not see death" (Heb. 11:5). This means he was raptured. He was not on the earth anymore because God took him.

Even though Enoch's life was outwardly like that of everyone around him, God took only him. There was something special about him that was pleasing to God (Heb. 11:5). He was so different, but not in a peculiar way. His life was one of coming to God and seeking after Him (v. 6). This made him strikingly different from those around him. Though he lived a normal life, no one could understand or explain him. Inwardly, he was different. There was something about him that was pleasing to God. This is the second aspect of walking with God.

Our lives should cause people to think there is something different about us. When we walk with God, there will be something about us that others will not understand (1 Cor. 2:15). While others are trying to gain things for themselves, we live to please God. What we seek is different from what everyone else in the world pursues.

We are so normal, yet we are not common. When people are with us, they sense something different. The Bible uses the term "aroma" to describe this (2 Cor. 2:16). There is an aroma coming from us which tells people that we are not common. After just a brief conversation with us, they realize we are special. The way we behave, talk, and live is different. This means that, like Enoch, we are normal, but we are not. There is an aroma about us that people don't understand. They can't say we are not normal human beings, but neither can they say we are normal, because no one lives the way we do. We are not. This is what it means to walk with God.

When the Lord Jesus was on the earth, He lived a normal human life. People could approach Him and talk with Him. He even dined with tax collectors and sinners (Matt. 9:10). Yet at the same time, people wondered about Him. They asked, "Where did this man get this wisdom and these miraculous powers? Is not this the carpenter's son?" (Matt. 13:54–55). People couldn't figure Him out. They marveled at Him. This is the living of Enoch. When we walk with God, on the one hand, we are so normal. On the other hand, we are so different.

Enoch is a picture of the marvelous Christian life in the divine and mystical realm. It is a living that is so normal, yet incomprehensible to others. May we all have such a living. May we be so normal and approachable, yet so special and mysterious, by walking with God.

8

Seven Stages of Spiritual Learning

Laodicea and Philadelphia

All of the points concerning the line of life are for our experience, but to us, they may just be objective facts. We should remember what the Lord said to the church in Laodicea: "You say, 'I am rich, and have become wealthy, and have need of nothing,' and you do not know that you are wretched and miserable and poor and blind and naked" (Rev. 3:17). The problem with the Laodiceans was that they were preoccupied with biblical truths yet had little experience of them. This is why the Lord rebuked them. We are in danger of becoming like the Laodiceans if we know much but experience little.

The church in Laodicea was rebuked because the believers there thought they were rich spiritually and didn't know how poor they really were. Truth alone does not make us rich. We may think that knowing truth makes us spiritually rich, but when the Lord Jesus came, He came not only with truth, but also as a man (John 1:14). This is the principle of incarnation. Truth must be constituted into us. The principle in the New Testament is that the Word became flesh: "In the beginning was the Word, and the Word was with God, and the Word was God....And the Word became flesh, and dwelt among us...full of grace and truth" (vv. 1, 14). The Word existed in eternity, but the Word had to become flesh so we could experience God.

In the same way, the truth we know must also be incarnated in us before it can affect others. If we only have the truth as teachings and our experience does not match that truth, then its effect on others will be limited. What matters is not how much truth we know but how much truth we experience. We must ask ourselves, "How much of what I know have I experienced?" All of these stages on the line of life must become experiential. Only then will they become operative. We should tell the Lord, "I desire to grow. I am willing to pay the price to experience all these stages on the line of life."

The Lord told the church in Philadelphia, "He who overcomes, I will make him a pillar in the temple of My God, and he will not go out from it anymore" (Rev. 3:12). This suggests that some believers do go out. When they are in, they love the Lord. They may even be burning for the Lord. But then they disappear and are out. Why are they in and out? Because they are lacking in their experience of the divine truth. As a result, they also lack stability.

Truth Experienced

Biblical truth is for our experience. It should not become just teachings for us to know. When truth is merely knowledge, it can make us arrogant (1 Cor. 8:1). The Lord Jesus said, "You will know the truth, and the truth will make you free" (John 8:32). Knowing the truth involves experiencing it. Truth only sets us free when it becomes experiential. Every biblical truth we know must eventually become our experience and reality. This includes all of the stages on the line of life.

Seth—A Realm

These experiences are all within a realm represented by Seth, the appointed son of Adam. We, as believers in Christ, have been transferred into this divine and mystical realm. Our experiences of all the stages on the line of life substantiate this realm. These stages are represented by the generations beginning with Enosh and ending with Noah.

The fifth generation was Enoch, whose name means "instructed" (Potts, p. 83). The line of life includes learning. To fully learn the spiritual lessons on the line of life, we need the experience of all the generations in this line. The real spiritual learning comes stage after stage.

Enosh—Weak and Mortal

The first generation on the line of life is Enosh, whose name means "a miserable man; a mortal" (Potts, p. 83). He represents the weakness of man. The Spirit enlightens us and exposes us until we see that we are Enosh—weak and mortal. Through this, we realize how much we need God's mercy. This is our first stage of learning.

Kenan—Gaining Christ

The second generation on the line of life is Kenan, whose name means "a possessor" (Potts, p. 60). This second stage of learning is the possessing of Christ by gaining Him (Phil. 3:8). The gaining of Christ comes through the realization of our weakness. To have the real learning, we must proceed from the first stage to the second.

Having our weakness exposed does not guarantee that we will gain Christ. For many, the exposing of their weakness leads to worry, concern, and regret. They grieve about how fragile they are. However, the Spirit does not enlighten us and expose our weakness so we can grieve, worry, or be concerned. Our weakness should turn us to Christ so we can gain Him. This is our second stage of learning.

Mahalalel—Praising the Father

The third generation on the line of life is Mahalalel, whose name means "praising God" (Potts, 160). The first three stages of learning are for us to know and experience the triune God. With these three persons—Enosh, Kenan, and Mahalalel—we have the enlightening work of God the Spirit, the gaining of God the Son, and our praising of God the Father. After passing through these three stages, we realize God's splendor. This is our third stage of learning.

Jared—Learning to Descend

After all these experiences, we come to the fourth generation, Jared, whose name means "descended; descent" (Potts, p. 129). After all our experiences of the triune God, in the fourth stage, we must learn to descend. Even after we experience God's splendor, we should not consider ourselves to be so high. We must learn to descend. We shouldn't remain in the riches of the triune God in such a way that we become peculiar. After we have gained so much of the riches of Christ in the first three stages, we must learn how to descend and be normal. We must learn how to be with all kinds of people. This is the fourth stage of learning.

Enoch—Learning and Bearing Responsibility

The fifth generation on the line of life is Enoch, whose name means "instructed" (Potts, p. 83). Enoch represents learning, and with learning comes responsibility.

This Enoch is different from the Enoch on the line of knowledge. Both of them represent learning, but the learning on the line of knowledge is objective and doctrinal, while that on the line of life is subjective and experiential. The learning on Cain's line comes quickly and easily, but that on Seth's line is slower and at a cost. What we learn on the line of life becomes a controlling vision that regulates our living. We are responsible for what we see. This is the experience of Enoch on the line of life, our fifth stage of learning.

Methuselah—Living for the Lord's Return

"Enoch lived sixty-five years, and became the father of Methuselah" (Gen. 5:21). Methuselah means "sending forth of death" (Potts, p. 171). No doubt, this name was based on Enoch's prophecy: "Behold, the Lord came with many thousands of His holy ones, to execute judgment upon all, and to convict all the ungodly of all their ungodly deeds which they have done in an ungodly way, and of all the harsh things which ungodly sinners have spoken against Him" (Jude 14–15). This prophecy has a double fulfillment, first at Noah's time through the judgment of the flood, and second at the Lord's return through the judgment seat of Christ (2 Cor. 5:10) and the great white throne (Rev. 20:11–12). Like Methuselah, who lived his life in view of a coming judgment, we should live soberly, watching expectantly for the Lord's coming (1 Thess. 5:2–10). In this stage, we should learn to live our life in view of the Lord's return.

In all of human history, no one lived longer than Methuselah (Gen. 5:27). He faithfully waited over nine centuries for the fulfillment of his father's prophecy. We also are waiting for a coming judgment. Our waiting is not motivated simply by outward signs of the Lord's return but by the desire to please our returning Master. Our expectation of the Lord's coming should cause us to live as faithful and sensible slaves, serving our Master's household (Matt. 24:45–51). Whether the Lord comes quickly or delays His coming, our attitude should remain the same—we watch and prepare daily. Our life is controlled by our expectation of His coming. We may be "alive and remain until the coming of the Lord," or we may have "fallen asleep in Jesus" before He comes (1 Thess. 4:14–15). Either way, our hope is for His approval when we see Him.

Lamech—Being Beside Ourselves

"Methuselah lived one hundred and eighty-seven years, and became the father of Lamech" (Gen. 5:25). Methuselah and Lamech, who were father and son, represent only one generation. Lamech died before his father Methuselah. The year Methuselah died was the year of the great flood. Since the son died before the father, they should be considered as one generation. Lamech is included in the generation of Methuselah, and they represent two aspects of the sixth stage of learning. If we count Methuselah and Lamech as one generation, then there are seven generations after Seth on the line of life.

Lamech means "powerful; wild man" (Potts, p. 153). How could a faithful man who is waiting for the Lord's coming be a wild man? God wants a wild Lamech—not the Lamech in the line of self who was full of murder and boasting (Gen. 4:19–24) but the Lamech in the line of life who was beside himself for God's will.

John the Baptist, who was looking for the Lord's first coming, did not wait passively. He was not polite to the religious people of his day but called them a "brood of vipers" (Matt. 3:7). He shouted, "Repent, for the kingdom of heaven is at hand" (v. 2). God needs Lamechs like this today, people who are strong and bold in order to be faithful to God's commitment, not caring who opposes them, willing even to sacrifice their lives.

God has allotted us only so much time. Our human lifetime is as mere handbreadths (Psa. 39:5), and the Lord may return any day. Today is the day to be wild for the Lord! We shouldn't wait until we are older and more experienced. We should heed the Lord's word to "be zealous and repent" (Rev. 3:19). As we await the Lord's soon return, may we all be beside ourselves, crazy for Christ and His church. This is the combined experience of Methuselah and Lamech, the sixth stage of learning on the line of life.

Noah—Resting in God

"Lamech lived one hundred and eighty-two years, and became the father of a son. Now he called his name Noah, saying, 'This one will give us rest from our work and from the toil of our hands'" (Gen. 5:28–29). Noah means "rest; repose; consolation" (Potts, p. 185).

Just as the seven days of creation end with a day of rest, the seven stages of learning in the line of life end with Noah, the one who "will give us rest from our work and from the toil of our hands" (Gen. 5:29). He represents the climax of these stages.

Noah labored diligently to build the ark as God commanded him. He must have had confidence and peace that his labor would bring about the fulfillment of the prophecy of his great grandfather Enoch. As he labored, he rested in God. Like Noah, we should labor diligently with the full assurance that it is not us but the Lord who does the work. The will of God can be fulfilled only through those who have such restful assurance. Outwardly we labor, yet inwardly we are restful. This is Noah, the seventh and final stage of learning on the line of life.

In our experience, these are not consecutive stages, but each one builds upon the other. What we learn in each stage remains with us and continues to be our experience. Through these seven stages, God blesses us with the riches of His grace and glory. These riches are ours to enjoy. May we live in the line of life. As we experience all of these stages, we substantiate the divine and mystical realm into which we have been transferred.

Works Cited

Potts, Cyrus A. *Dictionary of Bible Proper Names*. New York: The Abingdon Press, 1922.

Smith, William. *Smith's Bible Dictionary*. Peabody, MA: Hendrickson Publishers, Inc., 2000.

Online Ministry by Titus Chu

MinistryMessages.org is the online archive for the ministry of Titus Chu. This includes audio messages, articles, and books in PDF format, all of which are available as free downloads.

FellowshipJournal.org is an online magazine that features recent sharing by Titus Chu. It also provides brief, daily excerpts from his ministry, as well as news of upcoming events.

"Daily Words for the Christian Life" is an e-letter sent out every Thursday. It features selections from the writings of Titus Chu. To subscribe, visit FellowshipJournal.org/subscribe.

Books by Titus Chu

The books listed below are available in print, Kindle, or iBook format. To purchase them, go to MinistryMessages.org/order. They are also available via Amazon.com and iTunes.

David: After God's Heart

Elijah & Elisha: Living for God's Testimony

Ruth: Growth unto Maturity

Philippians: That I May Gain Christ

A Sketch of Genesis

Two Manners of Life